Greatest Ever

Pasta

The All Time Top 20 Greatest Recipes

Greatest Ever

Pasta

The All Time Top 20 Greatest Recipes

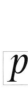

This is a Parragon Book
First published in 2002

Parragon
Queen Street House
4 Queen Street
Bath BA1 1HE, UK

ISBN: 0-75256-846-9

Printed in China

NOTE

This book uses metric and imperial measurements. Follow the same
units of measurement throughout; do not mix metric and imperial.
All spoon measurements are level: teaspoons are assumed to be 5 ml,
and tablespoons are assumed to be 15 ml. Unless otherwise stated,
milk is assumed to be full fat, eggs and individual vegetables such as
potatoes are medium, and pepper is freshly ground black pepper.

The times given for each recipe are an approximate guide only because the
preparation times may differ according to the techniques used by different
people and the cooking times may vary as a result of the type of oven used.
The preparation times include chilling and marinating times, where appropriate.

Recipes using raw or very lightly cooked eggs should be
avoided by infants, the elderly, pregnant women, convalescents,
and anyone suffering from an illness.

CONTENTS

INTRODUCTION

Versatile and adaptable pasta has been around since the days of the Roman Empire. It can be combined with almost anything from meat to fish, vegetables to fruit and is even delicious served with simple oil and herb sauces. No store-cupboard should be without at least one kind of dried pasta. Combined with a few other stock ingredients, it can be turned into an appetizing and nutritious meal within minutes.

tagliatelle

olive oil

large saucepan with lid

COOKING PASTA

Always use a large saucepan for cooking pasta and bring lots of lightly salted water to the boil. Add the pasta and 1 tablespoon of olive oil. Do not cover the pan or the water will boil over. Quickly bring the water back to a rolling boil. When the pasta is just tender, but still slightly firm to the bite in the centre, drain, toss with butter, olive oil or your prepared sauce and serve hot.

Cooking times

The cooking times given here are guidelines only:

Fresh unfilled pasta: 2–3 mins
Fresh filled pasta: 8–10 mins
Dried unfilled pasta: 10–12 mins
Dried filled pasta: 15–20 mins

BASIC PASTA DOUGH

If you wish to make your own pasta for any of the dishes in this book, follow this simple recipe.

INGREDIENTS

Serves 4 (makes 450 g/1 lb)
4 cups durum wheat flour
4 eggs, lightly beaten
1 tbsp olive oil
salt

METHOD

1 Lightly flour a work surface. Sift the flour with a pinch of salt into a mound. Make a well in the centre and add the eggs and olive oil.

2 Using a fork or your fingertips, gradually work the mixture until the ingredients are combined. Knead vigorously for 10–15 minutes.

3 Set the dough aside to rest for 25 minutes, before rolling it out thinly and evenly.

flour

tomatoes

eggs

tagliatelle

Coloured pasta

Pasta may also be coloured and flavoured with extra ingredients that are usually added with the beaten egg:

Black: Add 1 teaspoon of squid or cuttlefish ink.

Green: Add 115 g/4 oz of well-drained, cooked spinach when kneading.

Purple: Process 1 large cooked beetroot in a blender and add with an extra 55 g/2 oz flour.

Red: Add 2 tablespoons of tomato purée.

Right: When you make your own pasta, you can create traditional styles, or try your own colour and shape variations.

fresh herbs

garlic

INGREDIENTS

Pasta is the perfect complement to meat, poultry, fish, cheese and vegetables. If you have some or all of the following in your store-cupboard, fridge or freezer, you can rustle up a tasty, satisfying and economic meal at the drop of a hat – or at least in under 30 minutes.

Fish and shellfish

Pasta is a natural partner for fish and shellfish. Both are cooked quickly to preserve their flavour and texture, packed with nutritional goodness, and available in infinite variety. Jars of anchovies and clams or scraps of smoked salmon are invaluable for conjuring up pasta feasts in a hurry.

mussels

sardines

salmon

Poultry and meat

Poultry and meat are popular ingredients in Italy. Pasta dishes range from speedy mid-week suppers to sophisticated meals for special occasions. Minced beef, bacon and chicken are particularly useful.

garlic

Dairy produce

Cream makes an instant rich sauce for pasta. Cheeses, such as Parmesan, pecorino, ricotta, mascarpone, mozzarella and, less traditionally, Cheddar, are widely used for fillings, sauces and garnishes.

Vegetables

Pasta and tomatoes, fresh or canned, are inseparable. Spinach and mushrooms are good stand-bys. Otherwise, with more time to spare, almost any vegetable, from asparagus to courgettes, can be worked into a pasta dish.

Herbs and flavourings

Classic Italian herbs, such as basil, oregano and rosemary, are indispensable flavourings for pasta sauces. It is almost sacrilegious to think of eating pasta without garlic. Fresh, ground or flaked chillies pep up a tame tomato sauce magnificently.

Olive oil

Virgin olive oil is a must for cooking pasta sauces. It is also worth investing in the best quality extra virgin olive oil with the finest flavour when the taste of the oil is crucial to the dish.

chillies

red onions

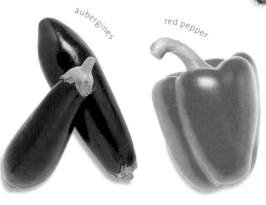

aubergines

red pepper

Below: A simple olive oil and fresh herb sauce transforms plain spaghetti.

asparagus

spaghetti olio e aglio

There are as many as 200 different pasta shapes and about three times as many names for them. New shapes are being designed – and named – all the time, and the same shape may be called a different name in different regions of Italy. Many are available both dried and fresh.

TYPES OF PASTA

tricolour fusilli

conchiglie

farfalle

anelli
small rings for soup

bucatini
small, long, medium-thick tubes

cannelloni
large, thick, round tubes

casareccia
long, thin curls with a twist at one end

conchiglie
ridged shells

conchigliette
little shells

cresti di gallo
curved tubes with a wavy ridge

ditali
short tubes

fusilli

spaghetti

eliche
loose spirals

farfalle
bows

fettuccine
medium ribbons

fusilli
spirals

lasagne
flat, rectangular sheets

linguini
long, flat ribbons

lumache
shaped like snail shells

lumaconi
big shells

macaroni
long or short plain tubes

cannelloni

minestrone soup

orecchiette
ear-shaped

penne
quill-shaped

rigatoni
large, thick, ridged tubes

ruoti
wheels

spaghetti
fine or medium rods

tagliarini
thin ribbons

tagliatelle
broad ribbons

vermicelli
fine strings, usually
folded into skeins

tricolour orecchiette

lasagne

tricolour ruoti

rigatoni

VEGETABLE-FILLED RAVIOLI

>Serves 4 >Preparation time: 35 minutes >Cooking time: 30 minutes

INGREDIENTS

RAVIOLI

450 g/1 lb basic pasta dough (see page 7)

1 tbsp olive oil

6 tbsp butter

150 ml/5 fl oz single cream

100 g/3½ oz freshly grated Parmesan cheese

STUFFING

2 large aubergines

3 large courgettes

6 large tomatoes

1 large green pepper

1 large red pepper

3 garlic cloves

1 large onion

125 ml/4 fl oz olive oil

3 tbsp tomato purée

½ tsp chopped fresh basil

salt and pepper

METHOD

1 To make the stuffing, cut the aubergines and courgettes into 2.5-cm/1-inch chunks. Put the aubergine pieces in a colander, then sprinkle with salt and set aside for 20 minutes. Rinse and drain.

2 Blanch the tomatoes in boiling water for 2 minutes. Drain, skin, and chop the flesh. Core and deseed the peppers and cut into 2.5-cm/1-inch dice. Chop the garlic and onion.

3 Heat the oil in a saucepan. Add the garlic and onion and cook for 3 minutes. Stir in the aubergines, courgettes, tomatoes, peppers, tomato purée and basil. Season with salt and pepper, then cover and simmer for 20 minutes, stirring frequently.

4 Roll out the pasta dough and cut out 7-cm/3-inch rounds with a plain cutter. Put a spoonful of the vegetable stuffing on each round. Dampen the edges slightly and fold the pasta rounds over, pressing together to seal.

5 Bring a saucepan of salted water to the boil. Add the ravioli and the oil and cook for 3–4 minutes. Drain and transfer to a greased ovenproof dish, dotting each layer with butter. Pour over the cream and sprinkle over the Parmesan cheese. Bake in a preheated oven, 400°F/200°C, for 20 minutes. Serve hot.

SPAGHETTI ALLA CARBONARA

>Serves 4   >Preparation time: 5 minutes   >Cooking time: 10–15 minutes

INGREDIENTS

425 g/15 oz dried spaghetti

2 tbsp olive oil

1 large onion, thinly sliced

2 garlic cloves, chopped

175 g/6 oz rindless bacon, cut into thin strips

2 tbsp butter

175 g/6 oz mushrooms, thinly sliced

300 ml/10 fl oz double cream

3 eggs, beaten

100 g/3½ oz freshly grated Parmesan cheese, plus extra to serve (optional)

salt and pepper

fresh sage sprigs, to garnish

METHOD

1 Warm a large serving dish or bowl. Bring a large pan of lightly salted water to the boil. Add the spaghetti and 1 tablespoon of the oil and cook until tender, but still firm to the bite. Drain, return to the pan and keep warm.

2 Meanwhile, heat the remaining oil in a frying pan over a medium heat. Add the onion and fry until it is transparent. Add the garlic and bacon and fry until the bacon is crisp. Transfer to the warm serving dish and keep warm.

3 Melt the butter in the frying pan. Add the sliced mushrooms and fry, stirring occasionally, for 3–4 minutes. Return the bacon and garlic mixture to the pan. Cover and keep warm.

4 Mix together the cream, eggs and cheese in a large bowl and season to taste.

5 Working quickly, tip the spaghetti into the bacon mixture and pour over the egg mixture. Toss the spaghetti quickly into the mixture using 2 forks. Garnish with sage and extra Parmesan if you wish. Serve hot.

MINESTRONE SOUP

>Serves 8–10 >Preparation time: 15 minutes >Cooking time: 1¼ hours

INGREDIENTS

3 garlic cloves

3 large onions

2 celery sticks

2 large carrots

2 large potatoes

100 g/3½ oz French beans

100 g/3½ oz courgettes

4 tbsp butter

3 tbsp olive oil

55 g/2 oz rindless fatty bacon, finely diced

1.5 litres/2¾ pints vegetable or chicken stock

1 bunch fresh basil, finely chopped

100 g/3½ oz canned chopped tomatoes

2 tbsp tomato purée

100 g/3½ oz Parmesan cheese rind

85 g/3 oz dried spaghetti, broken up

salt and pepper

freshly grated Parmesan cheese, to serve

METHOD

1 Finely chop the garlic, onions, celery, carrots, potatoes, beans and courgettes.

2 Heat the butter and oil together in a large saucepan, add the bacon and fry for 2 minutes. Add the garlic and onion and fry for 2 minutes, then stir in the celery, carrots and potatoes and fry for a further 2 minutes.

3 Add the French beans to the pan and fry for 2 minutes. Stir in the courgettes and fry for a further 2 minutes. Cover the pan and cook, stirring frequently, for 15 minutes.

4 Add the stock, basil, tomatoes, tomato purée and cheese rind and season to taste. Bring to the boil, lower the heat and simmer for 1 hour. Remove and discard the cheese rind.

5 Add the spaghetti to the pan and cook for 20 minutes.

6 Serve in large, warm soup bowls sprinkled with freshly grated Parmesan cheese.

SPAGHETTI BOLOGNESE

›Serves 4   ›Preparation time: 5 minutes   ›Cooking time: 1¼ hours

INGREDIENTS

3 tbsp olive oil

2 garlic cloves, crushed

1 large onion, finely chopped

1 carrot, diced

225 g/8 oz lean minced beef, veal or chicken

85 g/3 oz chicken livers, finely chopped

100 g/3½ oz lean Parma ham, diced

150 ml/5 fl oz Marsala

280 g/10 oz canned chopped plum tomatoes

1 tbsp chopped fresh basil leaves

2 tbsp tomato purée

salt and pepper

450 g/1 lb dried spaghetti

METHOD

1 Heat 2 tablespoons of the olive oil in a large saucepan. Add the garlic, onion and carrot and fry for 6 minutes.

2 Add the minced beef, veal or chicken, chicken livers and Parma ham to the pan and cook over a medium heat for 12 minutes, until browned.

3 Stir the Marsala, tomatoes, basil and tomato purée into the pan and cook for 4 minutes. Season to taste with salt and pepper. Cover and simmer for about 30 minutes.

4 Remove the lid from the pan, stir, and simmer for a further 15 minutes.

5 Meanwhile, bring a large pan of lightly salted water to the boil. Add the spaghetti and the remaining oil and cook for about 12 minutes, or until tender, but still firm to the bite. Drain and transfer to a serving dish. Pour the sauce over the pasta, toss and serve hot.

SPINACH & RICOTTA CANNELLONI

> Serves 4   > Preparation time: 10–15 minutes   > Cooking time: 30 minutes

INGREDIENTS

20 tubes dried cannelloni (about 200 g/7 oz)
or 20 square sheets of fresh pasta
(about 350 g/12 oz)

250 g/9 oz ricotta cheese

150 g/5½ oz frozen spinach, defrosted

½ small red pepper, diced

2 spring onions, chopped

150 ml/5 fl oz hot vegetable or chicken stock

1 portion of basil and tomato sauce
(see page 21)

25 g/1 oz Parmesan or pecorino cheese, grated

salt and pepper

METHOD

1 If you are using dried cannelloni, check the
packet instructions; many varieties do not
need pre-cooking. If necessary, pre-cook your
pasta. Bring a large saucepan of water to the
boil, add 1 tablespoon of oil and cook the pasta
for 3–4 minutes in batches.

2 In a bowl, mix together the ricotta, spinach,
pepper and spring onions and season to taste
with salt and pepper.

3 Lightly butter an ovenproof dish, large
enough to contain all of the pasta tubes in a
single layer. Spoon the ricotta mixture into the
pasta tubes and place them into the prepared
dish. If you are using fresh sheets of pasta,
spread the ricotta mixture along one side of
each pasta square and roll up to form a tube.

4 Mix together the stock and basil and tomato
sauce and pour over the pasta tubes.

5 Sprinkle the cheese over the cannelloni and
bake in a preheated oven, 190°C/375°F/Gas
Mark 5, for 20–25 minutes, or until the pasta is
cooked through.

BEEF & PASTA BAKE WITH PARMESAN

>Serves 4 >Preparation time: 10 minutes >Cooking time: 1 hour 5 minutes

INGREDIENTS

250 g/9 oz dried fusilli

1 tbsp olive oil, plus extra for brushing

4 tbsp double cream

40 g/1½ oz freshly grated Parmesan cheese

salt

fresh rosemary sprigs, to garnish

mixed salad, to serve

MEAT SAUCE

2 tbsp olive oil

1 onion, thinly sliced

1 red pepper, cored, deseeded and chopped

2 garlic cloves, chopped

600 g/1 lb 5 oz minced beef

400 g/14 oz canned chopped tomatoes

125 ml/4 fl oz dry white wine

2 tbsp chopped fresh parsley

55 g/2 oz canned anchovies, drained and chopped

salt and pepper

TOPPING

300 ml/10 fl oz natural yogurt

3 eggs

pinch of freshly grated nutmeg

METHOD

1 To make the meat sauce, heat the oil in a frying pan and fry the onion and red pepper for 3 minutes. Add the garlic and cook for 1 minute. Add the beef and cook until browned.

2 Add the tomatoes and wine to the pan and bring to the boil. Lower the heat and simmer for 20 minutes, or until thickened. Stir in the parsley and anchovies and season to taste.

3 Bring a pan of salted water to the boil. Add the pasta and oil and cook for 10 minutes, until almost tender. Drain and transfer to a bowl. Stir in the cream.

4 For the topping, beat the yogurt, eggs and nutmeg together.

5 Brush an ovenproof dish with oil. Spoon in half the pasta and cover with half the meat sauce. Repeat, then spread over the topping and sprinkle with the Parmesan cheese.

6 Bake in a preheated oven, 190°C/375°F/Gas Mark 5, for 25 minutes, or until golden. Garnish with rosemary and serve with a mixed salad.

MUSHROOM TAGLIATELLE

›Serves 4 ›Preparation time: 45 minutes ›Cooking time: 1¼ hours

INGREDIENTS

150 g/5¼ oz fresh white breadcrumbs

150 ml/5 fl oz milk

12 shallots, chopped

450 g/1 lb minced steak

1 tsp paprika

5 tbsp olive oil

1 tbsp butter

450 g/1 lb dried egg tagliatelle

salt and pepper

fresh basil sprigs, to garnish

MUSHROOM SAUCE

1 tbsp butter

4 tbsp olive oil

225 g/8 oz sliced oyster mushrooms

25 g/1 oz wholemeal flour

200 ml/7 fl oz beef stock

150 ml/5 fl oz red wine

4 tomatoes, skinned and chopped

1 tbsp tomato purée

1 tsp brown sugar

1 tbsp finely chopped fresh basil

METHOD

1 Soak the breadcrumbs in the milk for 30 minutes.

2 To make the sauce, heat the butter and oil in a pan. Fry the mushrooms for 4 minutes, then stir in the flour and cook for 2 minutes. Add the stock and wine and simmer for 15 minutes. Add the tomatoes, tomato purée, sugar and basil. Season well and simmer for 30 minutes.

3 Mix the shallots, steak and paprika with the breadcrumbs and season. Shape the mixture into 14 meatballs.

4 Heat 4 tablespoons of the oil with the butter in a large frying pan. Fry the meatballs, turning frequently, until browned. Transfer to a deep casserole, pour over the mushroom sauce, cover and bake in a preheated oven, 180°C/350°F/Gas Mark 4, for 30 minutes.

5 Meanwhile, bring a pan of salted water to the boil. Add the pasta and remaining oil and cook until tender. Drain and transfer to a serving dish. Remove the casserole from the oven and cool for 3 minutes. Pour the meatballs and sauce on to the pasta, garnish with the basil sprigs and serve.

CHICKEN TORTELLINI

>Serves 4 >Preparation time: 1 hour >Cooking time: 30 minutes

INGREDIENTS

115 g/4 oz boned chicken breast, skinned

55 g/2 oz Parma ham

40 g/1½ oz cooked spinach, well drained

1 tbsp finely chopped onion

2 tbsp freshly grated Parmesan cheese

pinch of ground allspice

1 egg, beaten

450 g/1 lb basic pasta dough (see page 7)

salt and pepper

2 tbsp chopped fresh parsley, to garnish

SAUCE

300 ml/10 fl oz single cream

2 garlic cloves, crushed

115 g/4 oz button mushrooms, thinly sliced

4 tbsp freshly grated Parmesan cheese

METHOD

1 Bring a pan of seasoned water to the boil. Add the chicken and poach for 10 minutes. Cool slightly, then put in a food processor, with the Parma ham, spinach and onion and process until finely chopped. Stir in the Parmesan cheese, allspice and egg and season to taste.

2 Thinly roll out the pasta dough and cut into 4–5-cm/1½–2-inch rounds.

3 Place ½ teaspoon of the filling in the centre of each round. Fold the pieces in half and press the edges to seal. Then wrap each piece around your index finger, cross over the ends and curl the rest of the dough backwards to make a navel shape. Re-roll the trimmings and repeat until all the dough is used up.

4 Bring a pan of salted water to the boil. Add the tortellini in batches, bring back to the boil and cook for 5 minutes. Drain and transfer to a serving dish.

5 To make the sauce, bring the cream and garlic to the boil in a small pan, then simmer for 3 minutes. Add the mushrooms and half the Parmesan cheese, season and simmer for 2–3 minutes. Pour the sauce over the tortellini. Sprinkle over the remaining Parmesan, garnish with the parsley and serve.

CHEESY PASTA SQUARES

›Makes 36 pieces ›Preparation time: 1¼ hours ›Cooking time: 25 minutes

INGREDIENTS

about 300 g/10½ oz thin fresh pasta sheets

6 tbsp butter

50 g/1¾ oz shallots, finely chopped

3 garlic cloves, crushed

50 g/1¾ oz mushrooms, wiped and finely chopped

½ celery stick, finely chopped

25 g/1 oz pecorino cheese, finely grated, plus extra to garnish

1 tbsp oil

salt and pepper

METHOD

1 Using a serrated pasta cutter, cut 5-cm/2-inch squares from the sheets of fresh pasta. To make 36 tortelloni, you will need 72 squares. Once the pasta is cut, cover the squares with clingfilm to stop them drying out.

2 Heat 2 tablespoons of the butter in a frying pan. Add the shallots, one crushed garlic clove and the mushrooms and celery and cook for 4–5 minutes.

3 Remove the pan from the heat, stir in the cheese and season with salt and pepper.

4 Spoon ½ teaspoon of the mixture on to the middle of 36 pasta squares. Brush the edges of the squares with water and top with the remaining 36 squares. Press the edges together to seal. Leave to rest for 5 minutes.

5 Bring a large pan of water to the boil, add the oil and cook the tortelloni, in batches, for 2–3 minutes. The tortelloni will rise to the surface when cooked and should be tender, but still firm to the bite. Remove from the pan with a perforated spoon and drain thoroughly.

6 Meanwhile, melt the remaining butter in a pan. Add the remaining garlic and plenty of pepper and cook for 1–2 minutes.

7 Transfer the tortelloni to serving plates and pour over the garlic butter. Garnish with grated pecorino cheese and serve immediately.

BASIL & TOMATO PASTA

>Serves 4   >Preparation time: 15 minutes   >Cooking time: 35 minutes

INGREDIENTS

675 g/1½ lb fresh farfalle or 350 g/12 oz dried farfalle

salt and pepper

fresh basil leaves, to garnish

BASIL AND TOMATO SAUCE

1 tbsp olive oil

2 rosemary sprigs

2 garlic cloves

450 g/1 lb tomatoes, halved

1 tbsp sun-dried tomato paste

12 fresh basil leaves

METHOD

1 Place the oil, rosemary, garlic and tomatoes, skin side up, in a shallow roasting tin.

2 Drizzle with a little olive oil and cook under a preheated grill for 20 minutes, or until the tomato skins become slightly charred.

3 Peel the skin from the tomatoes. Roughly chop the tomato flesh and place in a pan.

4 Squeeze the pulp from the garlic cloves and mix with the tomato flesh and sun-dried tomato paste.

5 Roughly tear the fresh basil leaves into smaller pieces, then stir them into the sauce. Season with a little salt and pepper to taste. Set aside.

6 Cook the farfalle in a saucepan of boiling water for 8–10 minutes, or until tender, but still firm to the bite. Drain thoroughly.

7 Gently reheat the basil and tomato sauce, stirring constantly. Take care not to overheat.

8 Transfer the farfalle to serving plates and pour over the sauce. Serve hot.

MIXED PASTA WITH PEAS & CREAM

>Serves 4 >Preparation time: 10 minutes >Cooking time: 10 minutes

INGREDIENTS

4 tbsp butter

900 g/2 lb fresh peas, shelled

200 ml/7 fl oz double cream

450 g/1 lb mixed fresh green and white spaghetti or tagliatelle

1 tbsp olive oil

55 g/2 oz freshly grated Parmesan cheese, plus extra to serve

pinch of freshly grated nutmeg

salt and pepper

METHOD

1 Melt the butter in a large saucepan. Add the peas and cook over a low heat for 2–3 minutes.

2 Using a measuring jug, pour 150 ml/5 fl oz of the cream into the pan, bring to the boil and simmer for 1–1½ minutes, or until slightly thickened. Remove the pan from the heat.

3 Meanwhile, bring a large pan of lightly salted water to the boil. Add the spaghetti or tagliatelle and olive oil and cook for 2–3 minutes, or until just tender but still firm to the bite. Remove the pan from the heat, drain the pasta thoroughly and return to the pan.

4 Add the pea and cream mixture to the pasta. Return the pan to the heat and add the remaining cream and the Parmesan cheese and season to taste with freshly grated nutmeg and salt and pepper.

5 Using 2 forks, toss the pasta to coat with the peas and cream, while heating through.

6 Transfer the pasta to a serving dish and serve hot, with extra Parmesan cheese.

LASAGNE WITH MEAT SAUCE & HERBS

>Serves 4 >Preparation time: 10 minutes >Cooking time: 1½ hours

INGREDIENTS

14 sheets pre-cooked lasagne

850 ml/1½ pints home-made or packet-mix béchamel sauce

85 g/3 oz mozzarella cheese, grated

MEAT SAUCE

2 tbsp olive oil

450 g/1 lb minced beef

1 large onion, chopped

1 celery stick, diced

4 garlic cloves, crushed

25g/1 oz plain flour

300 ml/10 fl oz beef stock

150 ml/5 fl oz red wine

1 tbsp chopped fresh parsley

1 tsp chopped fresh marjoram

1 tsp chopped fresh basil, plus extra to garnish

2 tbsp tomato purée

salt and pepper

METHOD

1 To make the meat sauce, heat the olive oil in a large frying pan. Add the minced beef and fry, stirring frequently, until browned all over. Add the onion, celery and crushed garlic and cook for 3 minutes.

2 Sprinkle over the flour and cook, stirring constantly, for 1 minute. Gradually stir in the stock and red wine, season well with salt and pepper and add the parsley, marjoram and basil. Bring to the boil, lower the heat and simmer for 35 minutes. Add the tomato purée and simmer for a further 10 minutes.

3 Lightly grease an ovenproof dish. Arrange sheets of lasagne over the base of the dish, spoon over a layer of meat sauce, then béchamel sauce. Place another layer of lasagne on top and repeat the process twice, finishing with a layer of béchamel sauce. Sprinkle over the grated mozzarella cheese.

4 Bake the lasagne in a preheated oven, 190°C/375°F/Gas Mark 5, for 35 minutes, or until the top is golden brown and bubbling. Garnish with fresh basil and serve hot.

GOLDEN SEAFOOD PASTA

>Serves 4 >Preparation time: 15–20 minutes >Cooking time: 25–30 minutes

INGREDIENTS

1 kg/2 lb 4 oz mussels

150 ml/5 fl oz white wine

1 medium onion, finely chopped

2 tbsp butter

2 garlic cloves, crushed

2 tsp cornflour

300 ml/10 fl oz double cream

pinch of saffron threads or saffron powder

1 egg yolk

juice of ½ lemon

450 g/1 lb dried tagliatelle

1 tbsp olive oil

salt and pepper

3 tbsp chopped fresh parsley, to garnish

METHOD

1 Scrub and debeard the mussels under cold running water. Discard any that do not close when sharply tapped. Put the mussels in a pan with the wine and onion. Cover and cook over a high heat, shaking the pan, for 5–8 minutes, or until the shells open.

2 Drain and reserve the cooking liquid. Discard any mussels that are still closed. Reserve a few mussels for the garnish and remove the remainder from their shells.

3 Strain the cooking liquid into a saucepan. Bring to the boil and reduce by about half. Remove the pan from the heat.

4 Melt the butter in a saucepan. Add the garlic and cook, stirring frequently, for 2 minutes, until golden brown. Stir in the cornflour and cook, stirring, for 1 minute. Gradually stir in the cooking liquid and the cream. Crush the saffron threads and add to the pan. Season with salt and pepper to taste and simmer over a low heat for 2–3 minutes, or until thickened.

5 Stir in the egg yolk, lemon juice and shelled mussels. Do not allow the mixture to boil.

6 Meanwhile, bring a pan of salted water to the boil. Add the pasta and oil and cook until tender, but still firm to the bite. Drain and transfer to a serving dish. Add the mussel mixture and toss. Garnish with the parsley and reserved mussels and serve.

SPAGHETTI AL VONGOLE

>Serves 4   >Preparation time: 10 minutes   >Cooking time: 1 hour

INGREDIENTS

900 g/2 lb live clams, scrubbed

2 tbsp olive oil

1 large onion, finely chopped

2 garlic cloves, finely chopped

1 tsp fresh thyme leaves

150 ml/5 fl oz white wine

400 g/14 oz canned chopped tomatoes

350 g/12 oz dried spaghetti

1 tbsp chopped fresh parsley

salt and pepper

METHOD

1 Put the clams into a large saucepan with just the water clinging to their shells. Cook, covered, over a high heat for 3–4 minutes, shaking the pan occasionally, until all the clams have opened. Remove from the heat and strain, reserving the cooking liquid. Discard any clams that remain closed. Set aside.

2 Heat the oil in a saucepan and add the onion. Cook for 10 minutes over a low heat until softened but not coloured. Add the garlic and thyme and cook for an additional 30 seconds. Increase the heat and add the white wine. Simmer rapidly until reduced and syrupy. Add the tomatoes and reserved clam cooking liquid. Cover and simmer for 15 minutes. Uncover and simmer for an additional 15 minutes until thickened. Season to taste.

3 Meanwhile, cook the spaghetti in plenty of boiling salted water according to the packet instructions, until tender but still firm to the bite. Drain well and return to the pan.

4 Add the clams to the tomato sauce and heat through for 2–3 minutes. Add the parsley and stir well. Add the tomato sauce to the pasta and toss together until the pasta is well coated. Serve hot.

PASTA & ANCHOVY SAUCE

›Serves 4 ›Preparation time: 10 minutes ›Cooking time: 20 minutes

INGREDIENTS

6 tbsp olive oil

2 garlic cloves, crushed

60 g/2¼ oz canned anchovies, drained

450 g/1 lb dried spaghetti

½ portion of pesto sauce (see page 29)

2 tbsp finely chopped fresh oregano

85 g/3 oz grated Parmesan cheese, plus extra
to serve

salt and pepper

2 fresh oregano sprigs, to garnish

METHOD

1 Heat 5 tablespoons of the oil in a small
saucepan. Add the garlic and fry for 3 minutes.

2 Lower the heat, stir in the anchovies and
cook, stirring occasionally, until the anchovies
have disintegrated.

3 Bring a large saucepan of lightly salted water
to the boil. Add the spaghetti and the reserved
tablespoon of oil and cook for 8–10 minutes, or
according to the instructions on the packet,
until tender, but still firm to the bite.

4 Add the pesto sauce and chopped oregano to
the anchovy mixture, then season with pepper
to taste.

5 Drain the spaghetti, using a slotted spoon,
and transfer to a warm serving dish. Pour the
pesto and anchovy mixture over the spaghetti
and sprinkle over the grated Parmesan cheese.

6 Garnish with oregano sprigs and serve with
extra cheese.

PASTA & PRAWN PARCELS

>Serves 4   >Preparation time: 15 minutes   >Cooking time: 15–20 minutes

INGREDIENTS

450 g/1 lb dried fettuccine

1 portion of pesto sauce (see page 29)

4 tsp extra virgin olive oil

750 g/1 lb 10 oz large raw prawns, peeled and deveined

2 garlic cloves, crushed

125 ml/4 fl oz dry white wine

salt and pepper

METHOD

1 Cut out four 30-cm/12-inch squares of greaseproof paper.

2 Bring a pan of lightly salted water to the boil. Add the fettuccine and cook for 2–3 minutes, until just softened. Drain and set aside.

3 Mix together the fettuccine and half of the pesto sauce. Spread out the paper squares and put 1 teaspoon of olive oil in the middle of each. Divide the fettuccine between the squares, then divide the prawns and place on top of the fettuccine.

4 Mix together the remaining pesto sauce and the garlic and spoon it over the prawns. Season each parcel with salt and pepper and sprinkle with the wine.

5 Dampen the edges of the greaseproof paper and wrap the parcels loosely, twisting the edges to seal.

6 Place the parcels on a baking tray and bake them in a preheated oven, 200°C/400°F/Gas Mark 6, for 10–15 minutes. Transfer the parcels to individual serving plates and serve hot.

SMOKED SALMON SPAGHETTI

>Serves 4 >Preparation time: 5 minutes >Cooking time: 10 minutes

INGREDIENTS

450 g/1 lb dried buckwheat spaghetti

2 tbsp olive oil

300 ml/10 fl oz double cream

150 ml/5 fl oz whisky or brandy

125 g/4¼ oz smoked salmon

pinch of cayenne pepper

2 tbsp chopped fresh coriander or parsley

85 g/3 oz feta cheese, well drained and crumbled

pepper

fresh coriander or parsley leaves, to garnish

METHOD

1 Bring a large pan of lightly salted water to the boil. Add the spaghetti and 1 tablespoon of the olive oil and cook until tender, but still firm to the bite. Drain the spaghetti, return to the pan and sprinkle over the remaining olive oil. Cover, shake the pan, set aside and keep warm.

2 Pour the cream into a small saucepan and bring to simmering point, but do not allow it to boil. Pour the whisky or brandy into another small saucepan and bring to simmering point, but do not allow it to boil. Remove both pans from the heat and mix together the cream and whisky or brandy.

3 Cut the smoked salmon into thin strips and add to the cream mixture. Season to taste with cayenne and black pepper. Just before serving, stir in the chopped fresh coriander or parsley.

4 Transfer the spaghetti to a warm serving dish, pour over the sauce and toss thoroughly with 2 large forks. Scatter over the crumbled feta cheese, garnish with the coriander or parsley leaves and serve hot.

PASTA WITH CLASSIC PESTO SAUCE

>Serves 4   >Preparation time: 15 minutes   >Cooking time: 10 minutes

INGREDIENTS

675 g/1 lb 8 oz fresh casareccia or 350 g/12 oz dried casareccia

PESTO SAUCE

about 40 fresh basil leaves, washed and dried

3 garlic cloves, crushed

25 g/1 oz pine kernels

50 g/1¼ oz Parmesan cheese, finely grated

2–3 tbsp extra virgin olive oil

salt and pepper

METHOD

1 To make the pesto sauce, rinse the basil leaves and pat them dry with kitchen paper.

2 Put the basil leaves, garlic, pine kernels and grated Parmesan into a food processor and blend for about 30 seconds or until smooth. Alternatively, pound the ingredients by hand, using a mortar and pestle.

3 If you are using a food processor, keep the motor running and slowly add the olive oil. Alternatively, add the oil drop by drop while stirring briskly. Season with salt and pepper.

4 Meanwhile, cook the pasta in a saucepan of boiling water until it is tender, but still firm to the bite. Drain thoroughly.

5 Toss the pesto sauce into the pasta to mix well, and serve hot.

29

SPAGHETTI OLIO E AGLIO

> Serves 4   > Preparation time: 5 minutes   > Cooking time: 5–8 minutes

INGREDIENTS

125 ml/4 fl oz olive oil

3 garlic cloves, crushed

450 g/1 lb fresh spaghetti

3 tbsp roughly chopped fresh parsley

salt and pepper

METHOD

1 Reserve 1 tablespoon of the olive oil and heat the remainder in a medium saucepan. Add the garlic and a pinch of salt and cook over a low heat, stirring constantly, until golden brown, then remove the pan from the heat. Do not allow the garlic to burn as it will taint the flavour. (If it does burn, you will have to start all over again.)

2 Meanwhile, bring a large saucepan of lightly salted water to the boil. Add the spaghetti and the reserved olive oil to the pan and cook for 2–3 minutes, or until tender, but still firm to the bite. Drain the spaghetti thoroughly and return to the pan.

3 Add the oil and garlic mixture to the spaghetti and toss to coat thoroughly. Season with pepper, add the chopped fresh parsley and toss to coat again.

4 Transfer the spaghetti to a warm serving dish and serve hot.

SPAGHETTI WITH ITALIAN MEATBALLS

>Serves 4   >Preparation time: 10 minutes   >Cooking time: 1 hour 10 minutes

INGREDIENTS

150 g/5½ oz fresh brown breadcrumbs

150 ml/5 fl oz milk

2 tbsp butter

25 g/1 oz wholemeal flour

200 ml/7 fl oz beef stock

400 g/14 oz canned chopped tomatoes

2 tbsp tomato purée

1 tsp sugar

1 tbsp finely chopped fresh tarragon

1 large onion, chopped

450 g/1 lb minced steak

1 tsp paprika

4 tbsp olive oil

450 g/1 lb fresh spaghetti

salt and pepper

fresh tarragon sprigs, to garnish

METHOD

1 Place the breadcrumbs in a bowl, add the milk and set aside to soak for 30 minutes.

2 Meanwhile, melt 1 tablespoon of butter in a pan. Add the flour and cook, stirring, for 2 minutes. Gradually stir in the stock and cook, stirring, for a further 5 minutes. Add the tomatoes, tomato purée, sugar and tarragon. Season well and simmer for 25 minutes.

3 Mix the onion, steak and paprika into the breadcrumbs, season, and shape into 14 balls. Heat the oil and remaining butter in a frying pan and fry the meatballs until browned. Place them in a deep casserole, pour over the tomato mixture, cover and bake in a preheated oven, 180°C/350°F/Gas Mark 4, for 25 minutes.

4 Bring a large saucepan of lightly salted water to the boil. Add the spaghetti, bring back to the boil and cook for 2–3 minutes, until tender but still firm to the bite.

5 Meanwhile, remove the meatballs from the oven and allow them to cool for 3 minutes. Serve the meatballs and their sauce with the spaghetti, garnished with tarragon sprigs.

INDEX